Banks

Margaret Hall

Heinemann
LIBRARY

www.heinemann.co.uk/library
Visit our website to find out more information about Heinemann Library books.

To order:
☎ Phone 44 (0)1865 888066
🖹 Send a fax to 44 (0)1865 314091
💻 Visit the Heinemann Bookshop at www.heinemann.co.uk/library to browse our catalogue and order online.

Edited by Charlotte Guillain and Catherine Veitch
Designed by Kim Miracle, Victoria Bevan and
    AMR Design Ltd
Illustrated by Mark Preston
Picture research by Hannah Taylor
Production: Victoria Fitzgerald

Originated by DOT Gradations Ltd
Printed and bound in China by Leo Paper Group

ISBN 978 0 4311 1679 2
12 11 10 09 08
10 9 8 7 6 5 4 3 2 1

British Library Cataloguing in Publication Data
Hall, Margaret
Banks. - 2nd ed. - (Earning, saving, spending)
332.1
A full catalogue record for this book is available from the British Library.

Acknowledgements
We would like to thank the following for permission to reproduce photographs: ©Alamy pp. **4** (geogphotos), **5** (Colin Underhill), **9** (Tony Hertz), **10**, **18** (Bob Johns/ expresspictures.co.uk), **14** (Motoring Picture Library), **15** (Paul Collis), **17** (John Powell Photographer), **19** (ImageState), **22** (Paul Doyle), **25** (Alex Segre), **26** (Ian West); ©Corbis p. **11** (Brooke Fasani/Solus-Veer); ©Getty Images pp. **6** (Andrew Sacks), **21** (Zia Soleil), **29** (Kevin Cooley); ©Pearson Education Ltd/Tudor Photography pp. **12**, **13**; ©Roger G Howard p. **7**; ©Shutterstock p. **16** (Alexei Daniline); ©Wishlist Images 2008 pp. **8**, **20**, **23**, **24**, **27** (Harry Rhodes).

Cover photograph of a young woman using a cash machine reproduced with permission of ©Photolibrary/ I Love Images.

Every effort has been made to contact copyright holders of material reproduced in this book. Any omissions will be rectified in subsequent printings if notice is given to the publishers.

Contents

What is a bank? 4

A safe place for money 6

Bank services 8

Current accounts 10

Savings accounts 12

Loans 14

Bank cards 16

Working with customers 18

Working behind the scenes 20

Banking without a bank 22

How a cashpoint works 24

Keeping track of money 26

Bank statements 28

Glossary 30

Index 32

Some words are shown in bold, **like this**. You can find out what they mean by looking in the glossary on page 30.

What is a bank?

A bank is a **business** that offers services that help people use and save money. When someone keeps money in a bank, the bank takes care of it. But the person can use his or her money at any time.

People keep money in banks because banks are safe.

Banks might look different, but they all offer services to help people use money.

There are different types and sizes of banks. A bank can be big enough to fill a whole building. Sometimes people can use banks in other places, such as in the supermarket or at home on a computer. But all banks offer services that help people with money.

A safe place for money

A bank puts money and other valuable things in a special, safe room called a **vault**. A vault has strong locks and is fireproof. Banks have guards, locks, and alarms. It is hard for anyone to steal from a bank.

Vaults are safe because they have alarms and strong locks.

The **government** helps keep money in a bank safe, too. The government has rules about what banks can and cannot do with the money people put there. If money is stolen from a bank, people do not lose the money they put in the bank.

Special vans with guards take money to and from banks.

Bank services

A bank is a place to save money. Banks hold money for people and they let people have their money when it is needed. A bank is also a place to borrow money. When people need money, sometimes a bank can help them.

Banks use the money people keep there to help other people and **businesses**.

Important papers and expensive jewellery are some of the items people put in safety-deposit boxes.

Banks also have **safety-deposit boxes** that are kept in the **vault**. People can keep important papers and valuable items, such as jewellery, in them. Only the person who has the special key for the box can open it.

Current accounts

A **current account** is a bank service that lets people use money without having to carry **cash**. To open a current account, a person gives some money to the bank. This is called making a **deposit**. The bank then gives the person a **debit card** and a **cheque book** with **cheques** in it. A cheque is like a note telling the bank to pay some of the person's money to someone else.

People can open a current account by going into the bank and signing some papers.

People can also open a current account on the phone or using a computer.

People can deposit money into their current account whenever they want. They can also take money out of their account. This is called making a **withdrawal**. Deposits and withdrawals are types of **transactions**.

Savings accounts

People open **savings accounts** to help them save for the future. Usually, money in a savings account is money they do not plan to use straightaway. People can **deposit** or **withdraw** money from their savings account whenever they want.

Most banks offer different kinds of savings accounts to help their customers save money for the future.

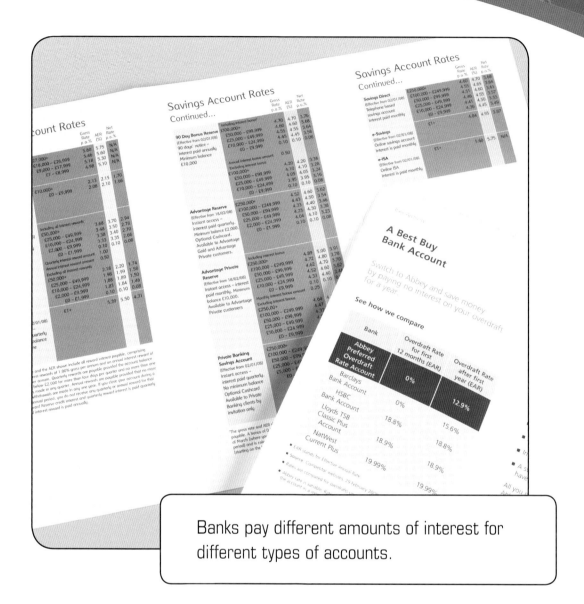

Banks pay different amounts of interest for different types of accounts.

The bank uses the money in savings accounts to run its **business**. In return, the bank pays savings account customers a special **fee** called **interest**. The interest is added to the money in the account. The longer money stays in the account, the more interest it **earns**.

Loans

Most people do not have enough money to pay for expensive items like a house or a car all at once. They can borrow the money they need from a bank. The borrowed money is called a **loan**.

Most new cars cost more money than people can pay at one time.

Loans must be paid back to the bank over a set period of time. In exchange for the service of borrowing a lot of money, the person must also pay the bank **interest**. The interest is added to the amount borrowed, so people end up paying back more money than they borrowed.

When people borrow money to buy a house, the loan is called a **mortgage**.

Bank cards

Banks offer special cards to their customers called **bank cards**. A **credit card** is a type of bank card that lets people buy things now and pay for them later. Using a credit card is like getting a small **loan**. If the money is not paid back straightaway, the bank charges the customer **interest**.

The interest rate people must pay for using a credit card is much higher than the interest rate for a small loan.

Debit cards look like credit cards, but they work like cheques.

Debit cards are bank cards that work like **cheques**. When people pay for things with a debit card, the money really comes from their **current account**. **Businesses** must pay banks a **fee** every time they use a debit card or **withdraw cash**. They must also pay a fee when someone pays money into their account. Banks make money from these fees and from the interest they charge on credit cards.

Working with customers

Many people work in a bank. Some have jobs helping bank customers. A **cashier** works behind the counter at a bank. Customers can make **withdrawals** and **deposit** money in their accounts with the cashier's help. Cashiers help customers to make all kinds of **transactions**.

Customers making a withdrawal or deposit must usually fill out a slip of paper and show some identification to the cashier.

Loan advisors try to get the best loan for each customer.

Banking advisors help customers to open new accounts. They can also answer questions and give advice about money. **Mortgage** or **loan** advisors work with people who want to borrow money from the bank. They ask questions and help to fill out the papers needed to get the best loan for the customer.

Working behind the scenes

Some bank workers do not work directly with customers. **Accountants** keep track of the money kept in accounts at the bank. They pay the bank's bills and keep records about the bank's **business**. **IT** workers run the bank's computers. Computers help keep track of money in customers' accounts and work out how much **interest** should be charged or paid to customers.

Accountants make sure that the bank has enough money to stay in business.

Customer service representatives do some of the same jobs that **cashiers** do. However, they also help people who choose to make **transactions** over the telephone, and they help people who call the bank with questions about their accounts. Security guards help keep the bank safe. There are many other workers needed to run a bank. In some way, every worker's job helps the bank to offer services to its customers.

Customer service representatives help customers who choose to do business by telephone.

Banking without a bank

Even when the bank is closed, people can use its services. They can do this with **cashpoint machines**. Cashpoints are found in many places, and they can be used at any time.

Cashpoint machines are found in many places, such as banks, shopping centres, and supermarkets.

Cashpoints do many things, including taking **deposits** and giving **cash**.

Cashpoints are linked to the bank's computers, so they can do many of the things a **cashier** does. Customers can find out how much money they have in their accounts and see how much money has come in and gone out of their account lately. They can also **withdraw** and **deposit** money using a cashpoint.

How a cashpoint works

A **cashpoint** works with a **credit card** or a **debit card**. When the card is put into the cashpoint, the bank's computer reads a code in a strip on the back of the card.

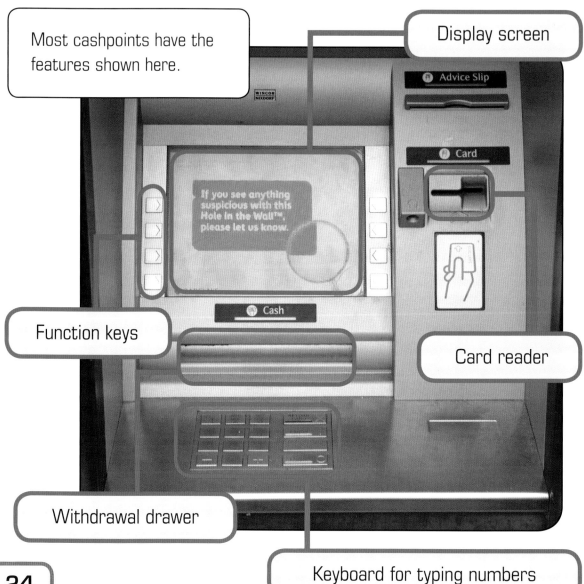

Most cashpoints have the features shown here.

Display screen

If you see anything suspicious with this Hole in the Wall™, please let us know.

Function keys

Card reader

Withdrawal drawer

Keyboard for typing numbers

The bank keeps track of everyone's transactions on its computer.

Then the cashpoint display screen asks the customer to type in a secret number called a **personal identification number (PIN)**. The PIN is a way to keep money in an account safe. It is important that nobody else knows this number.

Next, the cashpoint asks the customer questions about the **transaction** he or she wants to make. The customer chooses answers to the questions by pushing buttons or touching the display screen.

Keeping track of money

Banks keep careful records to show what happens to money. When someone **deposits** money, the amount is entered into the bank's computers. The computer records how much money went into the account. If a customer makes a **withdrawal**, the computer keeps a record of the withdrawal.

Customers can call their bank to talk about their transactions.

When people use a cashpoint machine, they can get a receipt.

The banks' computers keep track of every **transaction**. Even when customers use a **cashpoint machine**, they get a **receipt** as a record of the transaction. Also, customers are regularly sent a **bank statement** by post or on their computer. The statement describes everything that has happened with the customer's account over a month or a few months.

Bank statements

Customers should read their **bank statements** carefully to make sure that every **transaction** has been recorded. If there is a mistake, the bank should be told straightaway. Statements usually come through the post.

A bank statement, like this one, shows everything that happened with the customer's account in one month.

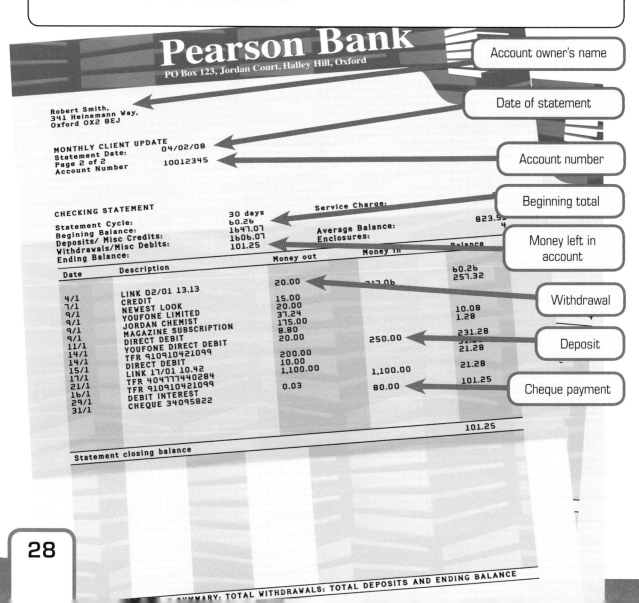

Pearson Bank
PO Box 123, Jordan Court, Halley Hill, Oxford

Account owner's name

Date of statement

Account number

Beginning total

Money left in account

Withdrawal

Deposit

Cheque payment

Robert Smith,
341 Heinemann Way,
Oxford OX2 8EJ

MONTHLY CLIENT UPDATE
Statement Date: 04/02/08
Page 2 of 2
Account Number   10012345

CHECKING STATEMENT

		Service Charge:		823.5
Statement Cycle:	30 days			4
Begining Balance:	60.26			
Deposits/ Misc Credits:	1647.07	Average Balance:		
Withdrawals/Misc Debits:	1606.07	Enclosures:		
Ending Balance:	101.25		Balance	

Date	Description	Money out	Money In	
				60.26
				257.32
4/1	LINK 02/01 13.13	20.00	?17.06	
7/1	CREDIT	15.00		
9/1	NEWEST LOOK	20.00		10.08
9/1	YOUFONE LIMITED	37.24		1.28
9/1	JORDAN CHEMIST	175.00		
9/1	MAGAZINE SUBSCRIPTION	8.80		231.28
11/1	DIRECT DEBIT	20.00	250.00	
14/1	YOUFONE DIRECT DEBIT			21.28
14/1	TFR 910910421099	200.00		
15/1	DIRECT DEBIT	10.00		21.28
17/1	LINK 17/01 10.42	1,100.00	1,100.00	
21/1	TFR 404777440284			101.25
16/1	TFR 910910421099	0.03	80.00	
29/1	DEBIT INTEREST			
31/1	CHEQUE 34095822			
				101.25

Statement closing balance

SUMMARY: TOTAL WITHDRAWALS: TOTAL DEPOSITS AND ENDING BALANCE

People who bank online can check their account whenever they want to.

More and more customers are banking **online**. They use the **Internet** to look at their statements. They have to sign into their account using a special **password**. It is important to keep this password secret so that other people cannot see their bank account. Bank statements are important because they help customers keep track of their money.

Glossary

accountant person who checks the bank's accounts

bank card plastic card given to a customer that can be used to buy things instead of using cash

bank statement record of what happens to the money a person keeps in a bank

business organization created to make money by selling something or providing a service

cash coins and paper money

cashier person who works behind the counter in a bank

cashpoint machine machine that lets people use some bank services without seeing a cashier

cheque note from the owner of a bank account telling the bank to pay money from the account to someone

cheque book booklet of cheques

credit card thin, plastic bank card that lets someone buy something and pay for it later

current account service offered by a bank that lets people use their money without carrying cash

debit card thin, plastic card, used instead of a cheque, that lets someone pay for something using money from their current account

deposit money put into a bank account; or, to put money into a bank account

earn to get money, for example by working

fee money charged for a service

government leadership of a country

interest money charged for borrowing money. Or money paid to people for letting the bank use their money to run its business.

Internet network of computers around the world through which information is shared

IT Information Technology to do with computers

loan money someone borrows

mortgage money someone borrows to buy a house

online connected to the Internet

password secret code made from letters and/or numbers

personal identification number (PIN) secret number used with debit cards and credit cards, which only the account owner knows. It is used to get money at cashpoints and to buy goods and services.

receipt record showing the amount of a transaction or how much someone spent

safety-deposit box safe box kept locked in a bank where people can store valuable things and papers

savings account service offered by a bank for saving money

transaction business deal done with a bank

vault room in a bank for keeping money and valuable things safe

withdrawal money taken out of a current or savings account

Index

accountants 20

bank advisors 19
bank cards 16–17
bank cashiers 18, 21, 23
bank computers 20, 23, 24–25, 26–27
bank guards 6, 21
bank statements 27, 28–29
bank workers 18–19, 20–21
banking online 29

cash 10, 23
cashpoint machines 22, 23, 24–25, 27
cheque books 10
cheques 10, 17
credit cards 16, 17, 24
current accounts 10–11, 17
customer service representatives 21

debit cards 10, 17, 24
deposits 10, 11, 12, 18, 23, 26, 28

interest 13, 15, 16, 17, 20
Internet 29

IT workers 20

loan advisors 19
loans 14–15, 16, 19

password 29
personal identification number (PIN) 25

receipt 27

safety-deposit boxes 9
savings accounts 12–13

transactions 11, 18, 21, 25, 26, 27, 28

vaults 6

withdrawals 11, 12, 18, 23, 26, 28